SIGNATURE

BY BETH HENLEY

D0862708

DRAMATISTS
PLAY SERVICE
INC.

SIGNATURE
Copyright © 2002, Beth Henley

All Rights Reserved

SPECIAL NOTE

SPECIAL NOTE ON SONGS AND RECORDINGS

An homage to Frederick Bailey

*Dedicated with boundless love and endless
admiration to Greg Grove*

SIGNATURE was originally presented at The Powerhouse Theater at Vassar (Dixie Sheridan, Executive Producer; Beth Fargis-Lancaster, Producing Director; James B. Steerman, Educational Director) by the New York Stage and Film Company (Mark Linn-Baker, Max Mayer, Leslie Urdang, Producing Directors) in Poughkeepsie, New York, on June 29, 1990. It was directed by Thomas Schlamme; the set design was by Anita Stewart; the lighting design was by Donald Holder; the choreography was by Jennifer Muller; the costume design was by Candice Donnelly; the production manager was Sam Craig; and the production stage manager was Edward Phillips. The cast was as follows:

BOSWELL T-THORP .... Kurtwood Smith
MAXWELL T-THORP .... Mark Linn-Baker
WILLIAM SMIT .... Carol Kane
L-TIP T-THORP .... Christine Lahti
C-BOY .... Damon Anderson
READER .... O-Lan Jones
TVP PERSONALITIES .... Jennifer Cooley
Edward Enrique
Stacy Rukeyser

CHARACTERS

BOSWELL T-THORP — 40s, an art philosopher

MAXWELL T-THORP — 30s, Boswell's brother, a Tank Bureau worker

WILLIAM SMIT — 20s, a splatterer from the CTZ

L-TIP T-THORP — 30s, Max's wife, Boswell's manager

C-BOY — 11, a homeless government ward

READER — 20–50s, a graphologist

PLACE

The play takes place in Los Angeles.

TIME

The year is 2052.

NOTE: Actors of any race who are suitable for the roles may be cast. Ideally, the company should be racially mixed, giving a cosmopolitan, universal feel to the play.

Sets, lights and sound should be expressionistic. We need to know, however, that we are in some form of Hollywood. Elements should be spare yet precise. The effect is a strange, chaotically horrifying, deathly beautiful, sadly silly world.

SIGNATURE

ACT ONE

Scene 1

The year is 2052. We are in Boswell T-Thorp's apartment. It is nighttime. Boswell T-Thorp, a man in his forties, stands in colorful pants. He is bare-chested. Bright squares are painted around his breasts. There is a small purple square in the center of his forehead. Throughout the following, he dresses. He puts on a square shirt, a square tie, square shoes, a square wig, a square belt, etc. His box attire should be shabby, well-worn. Maxwell T-Thorp, Boswell's younger brother, is in despair.

BOSWELL. *(Greeting imaginary fans.)* Good evening! Good eve! Everyone; all! I'm back; I've returned! Certainly the Box Theory was mine, all mine. I invented it. It came from me.

MAXWELL. Boz, I wish you could — I don't understand — I need someone to explain. Because, zap, zap, I love her so much.

BOSWELL. *(To imaginary people.)* No, I do not sign — I never relinquish my signature.

MAXWELL. Oh, why can't she love me?! What made her stop loving me?! I'm just me!

BOSWELL. Please, please, please! Can't you see I'm trying to get into the party mode?!

MAXWELL. Yes, of course. Go ahead. Forgive me.

BOSWELL. *(To imaginary people.)* Ho! Of course I recall it. The Box Salute. *(He does the Box Salute.)*

MAXWELL. It's all so funny! Because I thought it was good. But

7

it was not good. I was wrong. I was mistaken. A mistake has been made!

BOSWELL. I'm thinking you should leave. Tab some ear fuel and dust. I'm preparing for the party.

MAXWELL. No doubt you're a hobnob.

BOSWELL. Do you think I enjoy Hollywood? Do you imagine I revel in squealing like a pig? You must know how I suffer around the social screen.

MAXWELL. Yes, yes, of course.

BOSWELL. But a man must eat. There are price tags to be paid. Bills to be swallowed.

MAXWELL. Yes, please, you must go on to the Celebrity Chase. You must return to the limelight.

BOSWELL. I'm glad you comprehend. After all, tonight you are not on my menu. Now tab the fuel.

MAXWELL. *(Tabbing some ear fuel.)* They say this stuff'll eventually kill you.

BOSWELL. Yes, well, breathing will eventually kill you. *(William, a woman in her twenties, enters. She wears an orange splatter's suit, helmet and boots.)*

WILLIAM. Hello.

MAXWELL. Is this your tenant?

BOSWELL. Yes, yes. I'm forced to take in government tenants now. Look at this one! A splatterer from the CTZ. I hope you're satisfied. My only brother and you refuse to lend me more. I need more.

MAXWELL. The Tank Bureau's cut back. What can I do?

BOSWELL. More work hours; personal sacrifice; Lotto Dot! What do I care? Get me K! I need K!

MAXWELL. Please, stop harping. I'm suffering. *(Max clutches his heart in agony.)* My God!

BOSWELL. What?

MAXWELL. My heart is bleeding. Look, it's bleeding. Blood. Black blood. I'm dying.

BOSWELL. Hold still! Let me see. You are a swizzle-headed goat. This is an ink stain. It's ink. From a pen in your pocket.

MAXWELL. It's the pen she gave me. It's my moon pen. Oh, how can I live without her?

BOSWELL. What is your problem? She noosed you. She shuttled you. She broke your heart like a matchstick. Big fucking dose.
MAXWELL. I loved her. I love her. I'm loving her still.
BOSWELL. Fine. You loved her. Good. Go love somebody new.
MAXWELL. There's no one new I can love.
BOSWELL. Yo, yo, yo! Wake up! Love is cheaper than free. It grows all over your feet like yellow fungus in tent town. Love. It's nothing more than an archaic form of egotism. A tawdry reflection of all the holes in your own shredded soul. Be a human being. Forget about love.
MAXWELL. You're a monster.
BOSWELL. Rumba! *(The TVP [television phone] starts bleeping. L-Tip appears on the TVP screen. She is a tall, striking woman in her thirties. She is dressed in an array of ghastly-colored flowers. Strange antennas poke out of her headdress. She holds a portable TVP. She is looking at it, trying to get the picture of Boswell to click in.)*
L-TIP. *(On the screen.)* Box? Are you there? Boswell, puppetto? I'm below, are you there?
MAXWELL. It's her. Oh my God. My beloved. She's there.
L-TIP. *(On screen, waving two Day-Glo tickets.)* I got us floor one chase passes. I pulled every pony I know, but we're on the main rug. Helleew?
MAXWELL. She's going with you? She's escorting you to the great suckathon?
BOSWELL. Zap up. *(Talking into his TVP remote.)* I'm here, L-Tip.
L-TIP. *(On the screen.)* I can't see you on my TVP screen. Click in.
BOSWELL. I want to surprise you with my outfit.
MAXWELL. Traitor. Hoodlum.
BOSWELL. Nick off.
L-TIP. *(On the screen.)* Yeah? Well, what do you think of my outfit? Don't I look sin? I'm dressed as Pansy Martin. Watch this. *(She does an impersonation of Pansy Martin the Fantasy Puppet.)* "I just love t'eat my platter of tulips in the morning dew. Jacka, jacka, jacka!" *(L-Tip drops character.)* I make a good Pansy Martin, don't I?
BOSWELL. Brill, dear.
L-TIP. *(On the screen.)* Oh, you reindeer you!
BOSWELL. Look, I'll be right down.

L-TIP. *(On the screen.)* Well, click, click, Box. We gotta go slide, spill, splatter and burn! It's suck time. Jacka, jacka, jacka! *(L-Tip starts putting in some ear fuel. Boswell clicks L-Tip off the screen.)*

MAXWELL. She knows how to put on a front. You wouldn't know she was suffering. Unless you knew her very well, you might not be able to perceive it.

BOSWELL. *(Starting to leave.)* It's time for me to jack off.

MAXWELL. She's going with you to the Celebrity Chase?

BOSWELL. She's my manager.

MAXWELL. She's a rotten manager. You're her only client. You never work. You should fire her. Please, Boz, I wish you would fire her.

BOSWELL. I'll give it some thought. She does look ridiculous. *(Boswell exits.)*

MAXWELL. *(To William.)* I didn't think she looked ridiculous. Did you?

WILLIAM. No. But the real Pansy Martin has pansy eyes and there are real flowers growing from her ears. Different kinds. All different kinds.

MAXWELL. The real Pansy Martin is a Fantasy Puppet. L-Tip's a person.

WILLIAM. Righto.

MAXWELL. I don't know. It's a problem. She's going to beg me to come back. And I don't want to be hardhearted. But there are certain consequences she should face. She baked her cake. Now she can choke it. I'm a proud man. I won't just come crawling back. That's not how things work. Not on my screen. *(Lights fade.)*

Scene 2

The Celebrity Chase. We hear the clatter, conversation, music, etc., of a strange cocktail party. On the TVP screen we see askew images of a decadent party. L-Tip and Boswell enter exuberantly.

L-TIP. Boswell T-Thorp. It's Boswell T-Thorp! The Box Theory! It's very up. He never meant that we were all utterly, completely doomed.

BOSWELL. That's a general misconception with the Regular Folk! To Dotheads, Boxdom translated: boxed in; cornered; trapped; limited by your own mind, resources, physical being —

L-TIP. Oh, no, no, no no! Boxdom is up!

BOSWELL. The whole thesis is that one may put a box around anything: a circle; a rectangle; a triangle; a moving spill! If only the box is big enough, everything will fit. It's all so — so freeing!

L-TIP. It's freeing! Boswell T-Thorp, you are brill. You make me sin, and sin and sin. Have one more vial. *(She produces two vials of a red liquid. Boswell takes one of the vials. They are both aware that no one is paying attention.)*

Scene 3

Boswell's apartment. Later that night. William wears a green union suit. She sits on her mat shining her shoes. L-Tip and Boswell are heard coming up the stairway. William pretends to sleep. Boswell and L-Tip enter. They bring in an air of exhilaration and exhaustion. They have been to a big party. They have been doing drugs.

BOSWELL. It would all be so apparent, if only those neoswifts would go to Orlando Land and view the original Boxdom poster. Unfathomable so many know nothing about Boxdom!

L-TIP. A member of the Old Guard came up to you and gave the Box Salute.

BOSWELL. *(Doing a Box Salute.)* Yes, yes.

L-TIP. And the little, pasty man serving decorative crackers, he asked for your autograph.

BOSWELL. God, what a pathetically hollow practice that is.

L-TIP. Also, you made a remarkable impression on M. Raffeyelle Movet.

BOSWELL. No. Not the lady I swiped with my boxed hairdo?

L-TIP. Yes, I spoke to her quite a while, all about you.

BOSWELL. Me?

L-TIP. Yes. She has her own channel.

BOSWELL. That woman with the rubber nose has her own channel?

L-TIP. It's on the Rehab Circuit.

BOSWELL. Oh.

L-TIP. But she's got good time slots. And I think — well, she seemed very interested in having you on one of her shows.

BOSWELL. Me?

L-TIP. Yes!

BOSWELL. Which show?

L-TIP. The — well, it's called *The Whatever Happened To Show.*

BOSWELL. "Whatever happened to"?

L-TIP. Yes! They do very few celebrities. In fact, you'd be the only one on the show your week.

BOSWELL. I — I'm ill. This is an insult. Why, I'm not some out-fad Fantasy Puppet. I'm an art philosopher. What more do they want from me?!

L-TIP. They want you on the show.

BOSWELL. Never! Never! Never!

L-TIP. Look, I know what you've done. But you've been out of orbit for a very long time.

BOSWELL. I can't stomach it. Look who the Big Splash of the season is. That newcomer, K.Y. Von Ludwig. Him with his loathsome octagons and zigzags. He'd better hope he makes his mark before his hairdo unglues, the smug little toast.

L-TIP. Hey, now try not to unzap.

BOSWELL. I should have answered my fan mail; I should have consorted with celebrity swine; I should have been a grinning, glad-handing salt lick for the press.

L-TIP. *(Giving him a blue dot.)* Here, lap a blue dot.

BOSWELL. *(Lapping up the blue dot.)* So what else — who else would — would be on the show?

L-TIP. It's all toptip. *(She produces a list.)* We got: whatever happened to a clear blue sky; good clean fun; a day at the beach; the open-stove policy; bloodbaths in China; anti-gravity gowns; micro pets; the downfall of capitalism; the coalition of fetuses; vulture hairdos; and things that last.

BOSWELL. How much do they pay?

L-TIP. Scale.

BOSWELL. When do they want me on the show?

L-TIP. Well, two weeks from Thursday. I mean — if — well. There's one thing.

BOSWELL. What?

L-TIP. You're kind of an alternate. You and "vulture hairdos" are alternates, in case any of the other stories drop out. But they always do.

BOSWELL. Let me get this flat. I'm an alternate on *The Whatever Happened To Show*?

L-TIP. Well, for now. Temporarily.

BOSWELL. Maybe I'll just call the Euthanasia Hot Line.

L-TIP. Please, try to be up. Up is in.

BOSWELL. *(Walking over to the TVP.)* They do it for free now. Government dole. Of course, I hear the paperwork's appalling.

L-TIP. You know they have this new ultra surgery where you can get your face fixed into a permanent smile. They say smiling twenty-four hours a day does wonders for your emotional health, as well as your appearance.

BOSWELL. Maybe you haven't grasped this, L-Tip, but I'm nicked, I'm busted, my plastic is pulp. I don't have money for fucking smile surgery.

L-TIP. All right. Relax. That's what I'm here to remedy. Here, I'll turn on the galaxy satellite. There's supposed to be — *(She turns on the galaxy satellite. The screen lights up with a glorious view of the night's sky.)* Oh, look. There it is. The moon. A full moon.

BOSWELL. A cloud's passing over.

L-TIP. There's the Big Dipper.

BOSWELL. A band of stars.

L-TIP. The Milky Way.

BOSWELL. Luminous.

L-TIP. Boswell?

BOSWELL. Yes?

L-TIP. Are you available for sex?

BOSWELL. Um … no. I'm under surveillance.

L-TIP. Oh. I didn't know. So sorry.

BOSWELL. Nothing's definite. Nothing's at all definite.

L-TIP. Of course. Well, if you get a launch window, let me know.

BOSWELL. Sure. I'm sure I will, very soon.

L-TIP. Sin.

BOSWELL. What about Max?

L-TIP. I've made an appointment with Video Divorce for this Saturday. That'll be the end of it.

BOSWELL. Umm. Regrettable.

L-TIP. Yes. But he just — and we were — anyway, things don't always …

BOSWELL. Yes.

L-TIP. I have all these — and with him I never could —

BOSWELL. No.

14

L-TIP. Great moon. And stars. Always up there, right?
BOSWELL. I suppose.
L-TIP. Late. Better go.
BOSWELL. Good night.
L-TIP. I'll let you know about the show. Shine on, Boxey. Jacka, jacka, jacka. *(She exits. Boswell stares up at the stars. William sits up in bed.)*
WILLIAM. Can I mix you your concoction?
BOSWELL. Yes. *(William gets up and goes to mix Boswell his medical concoction.)*
WILLIAM. I just wanna know — at the party? What kinda food did they serve to eat?
BOSWELL. I don't really recall.
WILLIAM. Was it the pretty food?
BOSWELL. I suppose.
WILLIAM. Tell me.
BOSWELL. I'm really not interested.
WILLIAM. Here's your concoction.
BOSWELL. Thanks. *(Boswell drinks the concoction.)*
WILLIAM. I'm sure it will make you well. *(William goes to her mat and sits down, hugging herself with both arms. Boswell looks up at the stars, looks back at her, looks back to the stars.)*
BOSWELL. Why are you hugging yourself?
WILLIAM. I — just am.
BOSWELL. You —
WILLIAM. Huh?
BOSWELL. Umm.
WILLIAM. *(Softly.)* Oh. *(Boswell gives a nearly imperceivable nod. William moves over to his mat. Boswell keeps his arms folded. William sits near to him. She folds her arms. They do not touch.)*
BOSWELL. There were pink bubble shrimp served on a lavender platter surrounded by electric oysters. There was a marvelous blue dot dip; a crouton tray; some rainbow cheese balls garnished with yellow sea clover; sizzling clay steaks on a fried and refried tray; succulent duck bills ... *(As Boswell talks, William slowly leans over and sets her head on his shoulder. The lights fade. Street noises come up. We hear the sound of wind and trash being blown down alleyways. Strange animals are howling.)*

15

Scene 4

The lights fade up on the stoop in front of L-Tip's apartment building. It is later that same night. There are two filthy, ragged homeless people sleeping out on the streets (Reader and C-Boy). They stay huddled under their rags throughout the following scene. L-Tip enters. She starts up the stoop. Max steps out of the shadows. His face is pale and his hands are trembling.

MAXWELL. I just want to know. I want you to tell me. About my fingers. What am I — I mean — my fingers …
L-TIP. I'm not — I won't —
MAXWELL. Fingers on my hands. They're part of me, and yet they know where you dream. They've been all through you, journeyed up you and in you. I can never change where they have traveled.
L-TIP. There are parts of me — parts of my life, that have nothing to do with you.
MAXWELL. So you're walking right over me. Stepping on my forehead with your highest heel. Impaling my heart with your blood spiked shoe. I won't zap. I won't even squirm. Just don't — don't make that call.
L-TIP. We're morgued.
MAXWELL. We're not. No. Nothing is morgued. Not when I am willing to do anything. Any fucking thing. Stand here in the road and scream out your name. Lie down like a bog and let you kick in my brains. Or crawl, I will crawl; I will crawl at your feet. *(He gets down on all fours and starts crawling to her.)* I'm crawling. Come on. Kick me. I'm crawling. Kick in my gums, my lips, my face — whatever you want. I'm crawling to you! *(He crawls up to her and starts climbing up her legs. She kicks and shoves him away.)*
L-TIP. Get away. Leave me. There is nothing I want from you. There is not one thing that belongs to you that I would have. Not a

notion; not a smile; not the time of day; or a cut of gum. *(She stops kicking him. He looks up at her and wipes blood away from his mouth.)* MAXWELL. Please ... Forgive me. Please. This is not the way I normally behave. This is not who I am. I can't — I have never — and it is ... killing me. I wish, for both our sakes, I wish I was dead. *(Max gets up and exits. L-Tip looks after him. She clutches her arms around herself and leans against the stoop; garbage whirls around her. There is the sound of rushing water and wind. the lights fade.)*

Scene 5

The lights fade up on Boswell's apartment. The sound of a shower is heard from behind the lavatory door. It is night. William stands at attention before the TVP screen. She wears her orange splatter pants over her green long johns. She wears a crisp white bow tie around her neck, white gloves, a white visor and spotless white shoes. She is talking to an official on the TVP screen. William speaks into the TVP remote.

OFFICIAL. *(On the screen; reading from an official report.)* " ... rescue tab, par X; attitude par X; 129 O.T. hours." You could be headed for the W.Y. Badge.
WILLIAM. Thank you, sire. I intend to get it.
OFFICIAL. *(On the screen.)* Good work.
WILLIAM. Overall P.T. check, please, sire.
OFFICIAL. *(On the screen.)* One hundred and eighty-seven deuce.
WILLIAM. My tab shows one hundred eighty-nine.
OFFICIAL. *(On the screen.)* Let me reprocess. Oh, here it is, two of your rainbow ducks expired in tunnel release.
WILLIAM. I thought they'd make it.
OFFICIAL. *(On the screen.)* Nix. Good work, though. Good try.
WILLIAM. A personal request, sire. A click up into Freezer Dorm

380-T, beds 142 and 143.

OFFICIAL. *(On the screen.)* You're only on a two-minute window.

WILLIAM. Please, just whatever I got left.

OFFICIAL. *(On the screen.)* Approved. H.A.N.D.

WILLIAM. Yes, you too. Have a nice day! *(The TVP screen changes to a Frozen Dorm. Many children and a few adults lie frozen in white compartments. The camera focuses in on William's two frozen children, Bonnie and Tabell. Talking into her TVP remote:)* Hi. I'm here. I'm here. Mama's here. *(She walks up to the screen and touches her children.)* Oh, you both look so sweet. I miss you, Bonnie. I miss you, Tabell. Shall I finish the story? The one about the beautiful girl who ate the toxic apple given to her by the evil queen? I — *(The screen flickers with zigzags, then goes dark.)* Oh, oh. Goodbye, Tabell. Bonnie. Goodbye. *(William puts down the TVP remote. She carefully begins removing her whites and placing them into the pristine box where they are kept. The water stops running in the bathroom. The front doorbell buzzes, then we hear Max's voice over the door speaker.)*

MAX'S VOICE. *(Offstage, from door speaker.)* Hello. This is Max. I stopped by. *(William clicks Max in with the laser remote. Max enters. He is pale and sweaty. His clothes are rumpled and dirty.)*

MAXWELL. Where's Boswell?

WILLIAM. *(Indicating the lavatory.)* In there.

MAXWELL. I need to discuss something. A matter. With him. You're William, right?

WILLIAM. Yeah.

MAXWELL. They bring you in from the CTZ?

WILLIAM. Yes.

MAXWELL. They still got sheep there?

WILLIAM. Uh-huh.

MAXWELL. I remember sheep. Wool trousers; lamb chops; bah, bah, bah? They got you working down on the shore?

WILLIAM. Uh-huh.

MAXWELL. You Quake, Spill, Burn, or Splatter Crew?

WILLIAM. Splatter.

MAXWELL. Big mess, all that. Hard to contain. A real job for somebody.

WILLIAM. I do my best.

MAXWELL. This is not my day. I'm getting pasty. Meltdown. *(Boswell enters from the lavatory. His hair is wet and slicked back. He wears worn gray clothes.)* Boswell. I've come by.

BOSWELL. Yes?

MAXWELL. There's something … Well. You know, trouble. Some. Not much. That job I had — I don't. And I — lost my place.

BOSWELL. You're homeless?

MAXWELL. Who isn't? Really? These days.

BOSWELL. God.

MAXWELL. I'm gonna be dish. I got irons in the fire. Daggers in the air. Rain on the way. I just — temporarily — need a loan.

BOSWELL. From me? From me?

MAXWELL. You're my brother. I thought I'd ask.

BOSWELL. Look, I borrow from you. You don't borrow from me. You're the steady one. You earn the living. You know how that's done.

MAXWELL. I've been fired, noosed, chucked! They let me go!

BOSWELL. For God's sake, why do you pick now to have this metaphysical malfunction?

MAXWELL. She did it; L-Tip. She divorced me.

BOSWELL. Be that as it may, you cannot stay. You need to go. I have to eat my dinner.

MAXWELL. Please, I'm homeless. Couldn't you just … I could use anything. A tin cup. A cardboard box.

BOSWELL. I don't have any time for you. You have to go.

MAXWELL. Is it because of the monkey?

BOSWELL. What?

MAXWELL. Our stuffed monkey, Mr. Yips. The one our father microcharred, all because you wouldn't stop sucking your fingers. These two fingers here. He warned you. But you loved slurping them so much, you caused the torture death of our beloved Mr. Yips. That's why you hate me. Because I know you for the finger-slurping monkey killer you really are. *(Boswell turns to William.)*

BOSWELL. William, what am I having for dinner?

MAXWELL. Monstrous murderer! *(Max exits in a heartbroken fury.)*

BOSWELL. I posed a question.

WILLIAM. Deluxe Banquet Festival.

BOSWELL. I'm ready to eat. *(William punches a button.)* What are you having?

WILLIAM. Dotted broccoli. *(Two micro meals appear.)*

BOSWELL. Don't you ever get sick of dotted broccoli?

WILLIAM. I like broccoli.

BOSWELL. But you have it repeatedly.

WILLIAM. Sometimes I'll vary. I have cauliflower, or brocflower, or flowercauli.

BOSWELL. Never a dull moment with you.

WILLIAM. Every Sunday I have a sausage.

BOSWELL. I've seen that sausage you eat. It's a pitiful sausage. A sad little parsley sausage.

WILLIAM. *(Maintaining her dignity.)* I enjoy my sausage.

BOSWELL. I suppose it's all you can afford. You do the best with what you have. In a certain sense, you're to be applauded. Here, have a tomato.

WILLIAM. No, thank you.

BOSWELL. Come on, William. I know how much you like tomatoes. Go on, take it.

WILLIAM. I don't feel like a tomato.

BOSWELL. Don't be stubborn. Take the tomato. For God's sake, what is wrong with you? I'm telling you to take the tomato. I know you want it. Why are you treating me this way? For God's sake, take the tomato! I'm begging you, please, now, please.

WILLIAM. I'll take it. *(William takes the tomato.)*

BOSWELL. Fine. I just happen to know you like them. How was your day? Let's hear about your day. *(Quietly, desperate.)* I'd like for you to talk.

WILLIAM. Well, there was this sea lamb in the tubs out at the rescue center. Her eyes were sick and yellow and she was all covered in thick, black splatter. I put on my mask and gloves and started combing her with my furball remover fork. I combed and dug and scraped and tugged. It was tough going. Her eyes were frightened. This was a new experience for her. This furball remover procedure. But, eventually, I was able to scrape off most of the splat, and underneath I could see her skin was pink. A powder pink. I felt accomplishment, seeing that clean skin. It was a good day's work.

BOSWELL. A good day's work. My, how I've come to envy you, William. You with your non-skilled job. Picking lethal stickem off of dying plants and beasts. A mindless job, unglamorous, unrewarding, unbearably dull and useless.

WILLIAM. Some are saved.

BOSWELL. Saved? Saved for what? A miserable life in a filth-ridden world. One percent of one splatter is cleaned up before there is a whole new splat out. You save a thimbleful of sand on a blackened beach. You sit a legless dancer at a harp with no strings. Good work. Well done. *(About his dinner.)* This tastes like bile. I got the Final Report today.

WILLIAM. What did it say?

BOSWELL. It was unanimous.

WILLIAM. Does that mean?

BOSWELL. Yes.

WILLIAM. How long do you have?

BOSWELL. Awhile.

WILLIAM. A good while?

BOSWELL. Not really.

WILLIAM. A year?

BOSWELL. Maybe less.

WILLIAM. Less. I don't want you to die. To leave. You'll be gone. And I got to see you. Every day I got to see you. Where will they take you when you have died? I don't want you to be there. It's too far.

BOSWELL. Oblivion. I'll be in oblivion, where I'm sure I'll be perfectly dead and won't be plagued with any cares or woes. It's now, however, that's concerning me. It's now that's the problem. This time now when I'm alive and living with the burden of a mind, an imagination, and a trembling heart. Now, when I can lie awake nights picturing eons and eons of vast, dark deadness; where I'll be eternally alone, lost in nothingness without a book or a longing or a smile from some stranger's child.

WILLIAM. Boswell —

BOSWELL. I cannot. Stay away.

WILLIAM. Please —

BOSWELL. No.

WILLIAM. I want ...

BOSWELL. No. *(Boswell turns away from her. William stands*

21

alone, hugging herself. The chaotic sounds of the ocean roaring. The Reader, an ageless woman with fierce eyes, appears in space.)
READER. Come on. Come on. You wanna know? Come on. Up here. Eat with me. Mama took my cotton candy. But I found a wrapper. Pink sugar on the wrapper. Smell of peanuts. Smell of peanuts.

Scene 6

The stoop in front of L-Tip's apartment. Max, dressed in dirty rags, sits on the stoop. C-Boy, a boy of about eleven, sits on the edge of the curb. He is a filthy, emaciated waif. He wears an orange band around his waist and is eating from a government food box. It is an unnaturally hot day. The sun blares down. The smog is thick and green and brown. The chaotic sounds fade.

MAXWELL. L.A. has changed. I can't quite put my finger on it, but things are different. Things are — not so good. You may not realize all this. You're sitting pretty. You get a government food box every day. What'd you get in there this time? Any Fig Bolts? You get a Fig Bolt? *(C-Boy moves away from Max, hovering over his food.)* Hey, I wasn't gonna ask for one. I just wanted to see. Christ, I'm not even interested in food. Food! Who needs food? I live on poetry, poems and yearning. They flow from me like unkempt sewage. *(Max pulls various ratty pieces of paper from his pockets. He reads one of them to himself. L-Tip appears at the top of the stoop, carrying an air contraption. She is scantily-clad and is perspiring heavily because of the relentless heat. There are green stripes painted up the back of her legs.)*
L-TIP. Hi.
MAXWELL. Hi.
L-TIP. Hot day.
MAXWELL. Yes.
L-TIP. Here's the air contraption.
MAXWELL. Thanks.
L-TIP. I don't know how you're going to use it. You don't have

a home.

MAXWELL. It's part of the settlement.

L-TIP. Right. *(She turns to go.)*

MAXWELL. Hey, I was wondering?

L-TIP. What?

MAXWELL. Just — how are things with you?

L-TIP. Sin, really sin. I've got five new clients. And I'm right on the verge of persuading K.Y. Von Ludwig to sign with me. He's the Big Splash of the season, you know.

MAXWELL. So what makes you think he'll go with you?

L-TIP. You probably don't realize this, Max, but I'm starting to make a real name for myself around this town. People are calling me "L-Tip the Hip Lip." I'm really dishing up.

MAXWELL. Hmm. So this Von Ludwig's impressed with you?

L-TIP. Yeah.

MAXWELL. Oh, then he doesn't realize you're really a nobody. I mean, in the scheme of things. In this town.

L-TIP. He thinks I'm sin.

MAXWELL. Oh. What about you does he think is sin?

L-TIP. The green stripes I paint up the back of my legs. The ones you said were trash class. He says they suit me. He says I have legs like trees. Wilderness Legs, he calls me.

MAXWELL. What are you saying? Are you pogoing this toast? You out there hawking yourself like meat wrapped in tinfoil down by the fucking bay?

L-TIP. Look at you. You're curling up with jeally and you got no track.

MAXWELL. Hey, I'm not jeally. Not me. I'm not the type. And don't you zap labels on me. Don't zoom price tags on my forehead.

L-TIP. Chuck you. *(She starts up the steps.)*

MAXWELL. Hey, L-Tip. There's one thing I forgot to tell you. There's one big thing I lied about. Our whole marriage I told one big lie.

L-TIP. What?

MAXWELL. You are fat. You're a pig. Your thighs are pure blubber.

L-TIP. Bastard. You bastard. *(She exits up the stairs.)*

MAXWELL. I knew that would cut her to the quick. Calling her a pig. That was a good one. It got her. It made an impression. I don't really need the air contraption. It was just an excuse to see her. To make some headway. I wanted to read her my poem. I think she would have been moved. Oh, why did I call her a pig? What a mistake. What a misguided blunder! *(He slaps himself in the face.)* What now? What now? I guess, I'll just — have to — grip on. Right. That's all. Grip on. Next time it will go better. Next time I'll do things right. Next time I'll be the way I should have been now.

Scene 7

Boswell's apartment. Late afternoon. Boswell is anxiously sorting through a box of memorabilia. He is bare-chested. Gray sores are visible on his chest. William sits on her mat. She wears her splatter suit and helmet. She is cleaning black spill off of a strange creature with a wire brush.

BOSWELL. *(To himself.)* Very good. Very good. I must display important items from my memorabilia box. L-Tip will need to be familiarized with all facets of my career. *(Holding up a letter chip.)* What's this? Oh, a request for my autograph. *(Grandly.)* Someone once wanted a copy of my signature. *(There is a loud buzz.)* L-Tip! Darling, please enter.
JENNIFER. *(Over loudspeaker.)* It's Jennifer.
BOSWELL. Who?
JENNIFER. *(Over loudspeaker.)* Jennifer T-Thorp. One of your daughters. The middle one.
BOSWELL. Shit. One of my swarmy brats. *(Boswell turns on the TVP. Jennifer, eight, appears on the screen. She wears a kerchief on her head and holds a Blue Dot cactus.)* What do you want?
JENNIFER. *(On the screen.)* I brought you a Blue Dot cactus. Mum said you would like it.
BOSWELL. Oh, how shug. No doubt you read about my condition in the Up And Coming Obits.

JENNIFER. *(On the screen.)* Yes, we did. Can I come bring it up to you?

BOSWELL. No. Just put it in the laser box.

JENNIFER. *(On the screen.)* Oh. All right. *(Boswell clicks her off the screen.)*

BOSWELL. I'm sorry but I simply don't have time. After all I am someone whose face has been on a button. *(He holds up a square button with his face on it. A Blue Dot cactus appears in the laser tray.)* Here it is. A Blue Dot cactus. At one time Wanda and I had a whole garden of Blue Dot cacti. Poor Wanda. She doesn't realize how I've grown. *(He picks up the cactus.)* I don't want this. I'm throwing it away. *(William lifts her face guard.)*

WILLIAM. Could I have it? *(Boswell glares at her, then throws the plant into the receptacle.)*

BOSWELL. It's in the receptacle. Now get your clap back down. I've told you I can no longer tolerate the sight of your face. *(William lowers her face guard.)* You remind me of something I don't want to know. *(William goes back to cleaning the animal.)* And another thing. I'm getting sick of you bringing in these wretched creatures. Picking away at them all through the night.

WILLIAM. I want to get selected Worker of the Year.

BOSWELL. *(Sorting his pathetic memorabilia.)* God, how pathetic to live a life where every bone is a treasure.

WILLIAM. If I get the W.Y. badge, I'll be allowed a quarter cubicle. Then I'll be able to start the defrost on my kids.

BOSWELL. Forget about those kids. You don't know how lucky you are they've got them on ice. *(L-Tip's voice is heard over the door speaker.)*

L-TIP'S VOICE. *(Through the door speaker.)* Boswell? Hi. Hi. It's L-Tip.

BOSWELL. Darling, darling, darling. Entrée. Entrée. *(Boswell clicks in L-Tip. L-Tip enters looking more trendy and today than ever. She wears a dress decorated with packages of food and drug vials. She is uncomfortable visiting her dying friend.)*

L-TIP. Boswell. Hi. Hi. Hi … My, don't you … you look divine. I've never seen you so divine.

BOSWELL. Yes, and you're looking even more, more than ever.

L-TIP. *(About her dress.)* Isn't it sin? It's a fuel frock. Saves all sorts

25

of time. You never have to stop for drugs or meals. *(Offering him food off of the dress.)* Here, are you hungry? I've got Fig Bolts.

BOSWELL. Listen, L-Tip, I don't want your Fig Bolt, but I do have a proposal to make to you as my manager.

L-TIP. Whatever you want. Whatever I can do. *(Offering him grapes from her dress.)* Sure you —

BOSWELL. No.

L-TIP. *(Eating the grapes.)* I missed lunch.

BOSWELL. I just thought, in light of my present — state. That perhaps we could organize a salute to Boxdom. Something along the line of a Grand Memorial Dinner. Charge, say, two thousand K per tic. Get the elite satellites, get the V.I.P. press. The laser lead could read "Come See Box Before He's Boxed." I like that. It's thematic, yet witty ... What are you thinking?

L-TIP. Hmm. I don't know. Post retro is zap. Boxdom is a way-out fad. It's got no fangs for today's market.

BOSWELL. No fangs? I'm talking about handing you a dying artist's retrospective with the dying artist in tow, and you're telling me there're no fangs!?

L-TIP. If only you hadn't stopped so abruptly at the Box Theory. If only you'd done something more. Another poster; a grand prize.

BOSWELL. Yes, well, due to my remarkable intelligence, I realized early on this world was not an oyster I wanted to swallow whole. Thus I went on to other things. Like maintaining an image which was a vital part of securing government subsidy. I made replica posters, sold souvenir boxes. I did that ad for box perfume ... But I don't have to stand here and sell myself to you. You're nothing more than a noodle pusher who used me to worm her way into the Celebrity Chase. We went in there to get me work, me! Instead, you come out with five new clients, while I'm still standing here surrounded by the smell of zed.

L-TIP. Believe me, Boz. I've tried every sin in the book to get you a job in Hollywood —

BOSWELL. I'm not asking for a job. I'm asking for a dinner.

L-TIP. Don't you understand, it's trash class to give a Grand Memorial Dinner for yourself before you're really even dosed.

BOSWELL. Fine, fine. We'll just wait till I'm all dosed out, so we can leave it up to you to make me look good. You who have the infallible fashion sense to parade around town dressed up like a fucking Bee Jam's Supermarket. *(He rips food off of her frock.)*

L-TIP. Hey, those are mine.

BOSWELL. Goo Goo Pops, indeed!

L-TIP. You got no track!

BOSWELL. You're fired! You know that? You're fused! *(Boswell exits.)*

L-TIP. *(Yelling after him.)* Yeah! Oh, yeah?! Yeah! Ding-a-roo. Look, he tore off my snacks. I don't have to take this anymore. I got clients. I'm a professional woman. All my dreams are coming true.

WILLIAM. He thinks he's some big, fat bing. Well, he's not. If you wanna know the truth, before I moved in here, I never even heard of Boxdom.

L-TIP. Oh, it had its day. It lived for about as long as a fish can breathe in cement. But it's over, it's zapped, it's glue rot. He's not in step. I've got this theory. I've developed it.

WILLIAM. Yeah?

L-TIP. Trend is life.

WILLIAM. Yeah?

L-TIP. If you're doing what's doing now, at least you know you're doing something. Even if it's stupid and fleeting, dangerous or dull, at least it's happening. There's assurance in knowing you are participating in an era. Have some Red Dogs. *(L-Tip hands William some Red Dogs. Throughout the following, they eat and drink from L-Tip's dress.)*

WILLIAM. Thanks.

L-TIP. Before I had this theory, I wasn't anybody. All I knew about myself was I was in my thirties, I was Max's wife, I worked at a noodle stand, and Chee Chee Kitty was my favorite Fantasy Puppet. I had all the Chee Chee Kitty fashion attire, laser dots, kitchen equipment, toiletries.

WILLIAM. Moe Zoe Beam is my favorite Fantasy Puppet. But I don't have any of his stuff.

L-TIP. The thing is, all that stuff doesn't make you happy, 'cause you're still sitting on the sidelines. I ultimately realized, what I really wanted to be doing was all the things the real Chee Chee Kitty was doing on *Celeb Bites* — wearing outfits made of sugar stars, lapping up the limelight, dancing at Cafe Who's Who with Count Tidbit. So, for the first time, I decided to turn my life

27

around and become a manager.

WILLIAM. You just decided?

L-TIP. With every hair on my flesh. It thrills me knowing what I want, going out and getting it, taking it, swallowing it whole, wiping my lips and coming back for more. Mmm. *(L-Tip wipes her lips with her hand. William imitates her.)*

WILLIAM. Mmm.

L-TIP. Ya gotta slurp up the stars. That's why they're up in the sky.

WILLIAM. Go. I feel like a puff next to YOU.

L-TIP *(Showing her finger with a big laser ring on it.)* Tomorrow I'm marrying K.Y. Von Ludwig, the Big Splash of the season.

WILLIAM. Ding-a-roo. I saw his picture. He's dish.

L-TIP. Oh yeah, he's been on the front of five zill videozines this month. Of course he is unbearably conceited and self-sucking. But I don't think he can help that; he's Hot Splash. Anyway, this time I don't expect my marriage to work out. It's more like a career move. I'll do anything to get out ahead. 'Cause that's what I believe in. I mean, you gotta believe in something, right? Otherwise, what's the point? *(There is a loud banging at the door. Max's voice comes over the loudspeaker.)*

MAX'S VOICE. *(Over speaker.)* L-Tip, I know you're in there. They told me you're in there. Open this door. Open this fucking door!

WILLIAM. *(Overlapping.)* It's Max. He sounds like he's detonating.

MAX'S VOICE. Click me in! Now, for fuck's sake! Now! Click me in! *(He continues banging.)*

L-TIP. *(Overlapping.)* I'll click him in. I'll show him what for. Calling me a pig. Come on, you bastard. *(L-Tip crawls to the remote and clicks Max in. Max enters. He has a large cut on his forehead. Blood has dried on his face and on his dirty garments.)*

MAXWELL. You gonna marry that fuck?

L-TIP. Yeah, I am.

MAXWELL. But do you love him? You love that fuck? You think you're in love with him? It's — true love?

L-TIP. Yes.

MAXWELL. You do? You love that fucking fuck?

L-TIP. Yes.

MAXWELL. More than me?

L-TIP. Oh, yes.

MAXWELL. But you did love me? At one time? You did?

L-TIP. I guess. I suppose.

MAXWELL. But you stopped. It ended. You stopped loving me. Why did you stop? What made you stop? What? I — look, I've written poems for you. *(He pulls out endless poems, all crumpled and dirty, from his pockets, shirt, shoes, etc.)* All these poems. Love poems. Passion notes, erotica. And these! And this! And that!

L-TIP. What? What? I don't want these. I gave you love. You had love. You held its fluttering wings in your hands and crushed it slowly to death. Now you hold up its breathless body, look at it and say you're very, very sad.

MAXWELL. I didn't — I wouldn't crush — no — untrue.

L-TIP. Yeah, well, the whole time we were together you never stopped pogoing every woman who ever gave you change.

MAXWELL. You're the only one I loved.

L-TIP. Go. You didn't even know me. You thought you were married to Chee Chee Kitty. Remember how I always had to make those kitty whispers?

MAXWELL. I thought you liked that.

L-TIP. I thought I did, too. We were both wrong. *(She heads for the door.)*

MAXWELL. Please, tell me, I don't understand. What's happened to our love? Fourteen years of love. We were each other's lives. Can all that be wiped clean like dust across piano keys, and suddenly everything is silent? *(They look at each other speechlessly for several deafening moments of silence. Then L-Tip exits. Max starts to breathe heavily.)*

WILLIAM. You're bleeding.

MAXWELL. I — yes, I was hit by something. It was dropped on my head as I was walking down the street. A boulder, a Dr. Pop bottle, I don't know what? Something that could kill you.

WILLIAM. Did you hear the news about M. Boswell?

MAXWELL. Oh, yeah, in the Up and Coming Obits. Hasn't he always been the lucky one.

WILLIAM. It's not lucky.

MAXWELL. Maybe then you have something to live for.

WILLIAM. Sure. I do. I want a home to live in and I want my kids out of F.D. Then I want us all to learn to read and write and clap to music.

MAXWELL. May I use your TVP?

WILLIAM. Uh-huh. *(Max goes to the TVP screen. Max's click goes through on the TVP. An amiable woman dressed in white surrounded by pink carnations appears on the screen.)*

WOMAN. *(On the TVP screen.)* Hello. Euthanasia Hot Line. May I help you?

MAXWELL. *(Into TVP.)* Yes. This is Maxwell T-Thorp. I want to be euthed.

WOMAN. *(On the TVP screen.)* So you're calling to euth yourself, not a friend or relative.

MAXWELL. *(Into TVP.)* Yes. Correct.

WOMAN. *(On the TVP screen.)* Very well. If you'll just hold on a minute, I'll transfer you to the P.W. Department and we'll get started on your paperwork. *(Happy cartoons of people dying peacefully come up on the screen as Max is put on hold.)*

WILLIAM. Max, don't. Click off. Don't.

MAXWELL. I can no longer live caked in this awful pain. *(A rosy, pink man appears on the TVP screen. He sits behind a computer.)*

PINK MAN. *(On the TVP screen.)* Hello. M. Maxwell T-Thorp?

MAXWELL. *(To the TVP screen.)* Yes.

PINK MAN. *(On the TVP screen.)* We're going to need some information.

MAXWELL. *(To the TVP screen.)* Of course.

PINK MAN. *(On the TVP screen.)* Age?

MAXWELL. *(To the TVP screen.)* Thirties.

PINK MAN. *(On the TVP screen.)* Residence.

MAXWELL. *(To the TVP screen.)* Eighth box on Garbage Bag Row.

PINK MAN. *(On the TVP screen.)* Occupation.

MAXWELL. *(To the TVP screen.)* Unemployed.

PINK MAN. *(On the TVP screen.)* Reason for euth request?

MAXWELL. *(To the TVP screen.)* A broken heart.

Scene 8

The boardwalk at sunset. Later that same day. Sounds: ocean; wind; carnival noises; clean-up crews' machinery. There are two stools and a cardboard box set up. There is a sign on the box reading "Graphologist for Hire." Reader stands with one foot on a stool, hawking her talent. She has a moustache.

READER. One grain! One grain! One grain of sand. Magnified, magnify it. See if you can eat it whole. Time will tell. But I'll tell quicker. Let me read the writing; all the writing on your wall. Write your name on water. Sign your signature in the sand. I'll peek under your skin and tell you who's home. *(Boswell enters. He is distracted and pale.)* Hey, M.! Right this way. Over here.
BOSWELL. What?
READER. You.
BOSWELL. Me?
READER. You.
BOSWELL. What do you want, you filthy arrangement of molecules?
READER. I read writing. I'll read yours.
BOSWELL. I don't think so. *(He stands and listens to the ocean roar endlessly.)*
READER. *(Whispering to him.)* I can tell you who you are, where you've been, where you're going, what you need and what you'll get. For one extra quarter, I'll answer the big bonus question. You know the one.
BOSWELL. No.
READER. The big one. Why you are here. Why you're alive.
BOSWELL. I don't really think I need to know any of that.
READER. Suit yourself. But the truth is, you already know. It's all there, lurking in the writing. The handwriting. Look at the sunset. It's all green and gold and bloody blue. There's been a change in the atmosphere. A change in you.

31

BOSWELL. How much do you charge?

READER. Ten K. Plus a quarter for the B.Q.

BOSWELL. B.Q.?

READER. Big question.

BOSWELL. Oh. Well, why not? I have some time to spare. *(She hands him a laser pen that writes letters in the air.)*

READER. Write two sentences.

BOSWELL. What do I say?

READER. Makes no difference. Everything about you will be there. No matter what.

BOSWELL. Ha. This is silly. I've become a very silly man. *(He writes out two sentences.)*

READER. Now, sign your name. Write your signature.

BOSWELL. Well, yes. All right. *(He writes his signature.)* There. I've finished. *(He pushes the paper over to her. She reads it over with a stunning intensity. She looks up at him for a moment with dark dread, then looks back and studies the writing for several excruciating moments.)* Well? What is it? What do you see? What's there?

READER. *(She looks up at him.)* I'm sorry.

BOSWELL. What for?

READER. The sores are gray now, slate gray. They'll soon be red, then black, and then — you'll be dead.

BOSWELL. I — I — um.

READER. But that's not the worst of it. *(Referring to the paper.)* Your heart. It has shrunken and turned brown. You have a raisin for a heart. And your life. Your life is like an empty cereal box infested with microscopic bugs. Even in its heyday, all it held were Puffs. You're shallow, self-absorbed, antisocial, conceited, cruel and cowardly. You let a minute early success paralyze you into doing, holding and believing nothing. You're going to die unloved and unremembered. Why were you born? *(She rakes in the quarter.)* To prove how hollow and stupid life can be.

BOSWELL. I see.

READER. Please, I don't mean any of this as a value judgment. It's just — it's all right here. It's in the letters. It's in your signature.

BOSWELL. Where? How?

READER. Observe your shrunken L's; your twisted T-crossings; the cowardly crest dots of your I's; and the waywardness of your P's.

BOSWELL. Oh. Hmm. I — but how should they be? How should the letters be?
READER. It depends on who you are.
BOSWELL. How about, if you're someone who's lived — who's been — who is significant.
READER. Significant? Oh, well, everything would be completely different. The L's would be high. They would flow evenly. The loops would be daring and fluid, joyous and open.
BOSWELL. Show me. *(She demonstrates.)*
READER. Like that. See? Like that.
BOSWELL. I can do that. *(He makes an "l.")* How's that?
READER. There's no joy. You need joy.
BOSWELL. Joy. *(He tries again.)* How's that?
READER. Don't get frivolous. Think joy.
BOSWELL. *(He tries again.)* Joy.
READER. Closer.
BOSWELL. I must leave — I want to leave my signature. *(He writes his name with flourish.)*
READER. Very good.
BOSWELL. *(Encouraged, he writes again.)* Here lies one whose name was drilled in granite.
READER. Remarkable! That T-crossing! Such heroic importance!
BOSWELL. Then it's not too late?
READER. Change your writing; change your life.
BOSWELL. I can still know everything; do everything; be everything I have always dreamt?
READER. Ah, what a profound dot to your "i."
BOSWELL. *(Writing madly.)* All this time I didn't know; I didn't know I had everything right here in my hand. In my signature. *(The sunset turns blood red. Boswell continues to write. Blackout.)*

ACT TWO

Scene 1

Boswell's apartment. Max wears an intricately patterned robe and a turban with a jewel. He is reading the galleys of his book of poetry. Boswell is in a frantic state of exhaustion. He is trying to learn everything there is to know in the universe. C-Boy, who is wearing filth-covered rags and his orange government belt, is clicking images of objects up onto the TVP screen, and then pointing to various parts of the object with a laser stick. It is Boswell's task to identify the object and the parts. Each time Boswell gets a correct answer, C-Boy takes his pointer and hits the correct button which flashes and makes a buzz noise. Slide A is the universe.

BOSWELL. Good one. Good one. It's the universe. *(C-Boy hits the correct button, then Boswell goes on to identify the various parts as C-Boy points to them with the laser stick.)* Quasar. Quark. Doppler shift. Supernova. *(C-Boy clicks to Slide B. A clothespin.)* Okay, I know that one. That's a — it's a — clothespin. *(C-Boy buzzes the correct button, then points with the stick.)* Pinwood, gripping hole. Claw end. Spring slot. *(C-Boy clicks to Slide C. A nosebleed.)* Easy, nosebleed. *(C-Boy buzzes the correct button, then points with the stick.)* Nares. Nasopharynx. Leukocytes. Erythocytes. *(William enters. She is dressed in her splatter suit. She carries a pack on her back and limps slightly. To William:)* Hello, William. How was the reef?
WILLIAM. Cold. Freezing. Lost a toe. *(Throughout the following, William removes her gear. She takes off her boots and puts on her shiny white shoes. Her foot has a bandage on it. C-Boy has clicked to Slide D: pasta dishes.)*
BOSWELL. Go! It's pasta dishes! *(C-Boy buzzes the correct button,*

then points with stick.) Spaghetti Zog Puttanescan. Pasta Pickle Sarde. Tubettini With Porcini And Cream Dots. My favorite! *(C-Boy buzzes correct button.)* God, I'm a genius, a living genius. Oh, look at the time. I must rush to the Reader. Wait till she sees my new bounty. I have crossed a new plateau of penmanship. *(Handing C-Boy a list.)* C-Boy, when I return I want us to find the answers to these questions before dinner: How do you cook a fish? Who was Booker T. Washington? And is there a God or is this all just a free lunch? Well, gotta run. Jacka, jacka, jacka! *(Boswell exits. William and Max exchange looks.)*

WILLIAM. Zoom.

MAXWELL. Boz's handwriting teacher told him he must learn everything there is to know in the universe.

WILLIAM. Why?

MAXWELL. Because to know what he doesn't know, he's gonna have to know it all.

WILLIAM. Whew. *(Max shows her his manuscript.)*

MAXWELL. Look, they X'd over the galleys for my book. Here are all my poems in print. I'm very prolific.

WILLIAM. Go. And they paid you?

MAXWELL. Where do you think I got this charm suit?

WILLIAM. Things sure are going good for you.

MAXWELL. *(Clicking his fingers.)* Rumba!

WILLIAM. Maybe you should click up the euth line and cancel your order.

MAXWELL. What? No. I can't. The main reason they're publishing these poems is because of my back story. I'm the very first person to be euthed for love. I'll be remembered as the most romantic figure of the twenty-first century. I'll make history. It's part of the marketing.

WILLIAM. Max, I wish — please, don't.

MAXWELL. Look, before I was gonna get euthed I had nothing to live for. Now that I'm getting euthed, everything's going my way. Why rock the shuttle?

WILLIAM. I don't know, it seems dothead. It's dumb.

MAXWELL. Well, hey, I've got to take the bubble over to my publishers. They want me to do some video pub. Look, I'm sorry about your toe.

35

WILLIAM. It's okay. It was … a small one. *(Max nods and starts to leave again.)* Uh. Max?

MAXWELL. What?

WILLIAM. *(About C-Boy.)* Who's that?

MAXWELL. Oh, that. That's C-Boy. He's Boswell's ward. Don't ask me. Something in Boz's handwriting told him to reach out to the human species at large.

WILLIAM. *(About C-Boy.)* Well, what's wrong with him?

MAXWELL. Parents did a lot of ear slack. But he's all the Gov. would award Boz because of Boz's failing health condition.

WILLIAM. *(About C-Boy.)* Does he talk?

MAXWELL. Not to me. And he's really selfish with his Fig Bolts. See ya, Willie.

WILLIAM. Bye. *(Max exits. William goes over to talk to C-Boy.)* Hi. I'm M. William Smit. Do you talk? No? What was it, the drugs that got ya? That's a nice belt. It's orange. Red and yellow together make orange. I know that 'cause it's my favorite color, orange. They say the sun is orange. My suit is orange. My favorite food is an orange. I give myself an orange every holiday day. Maybe that sounds strange to you, someone giving their own selves a present. But I believe on occasions it's worthwhile to do nice things for one's self. For instance, I always try and keep my shoes nice and buffed. That way I know I always got something shiny to look at as I'm walking down strange roads that may not be going my way. *(C-Boy looks at her. He looks down at his filthy, tattered shoes. He spits on one of his rags and slowly starts to rub dirt off the tip of his shoe.)*

Scene 2

The boardwalk. The Reader is looking over the pages of Boswell's mad handwriting. Boswell sucks two of his fingers in crazed despair.

READER. More chaos! Worse swill! Such a vast bonanza of

garbage! Grotesque struggling, like vipers in a toilet bowl fighting to get shit on.

BOSWELL. Please, I wanted — I thought — is it too late?

READER. Too late for what? To race a rocketship to Mars? To dance with Ginger Rogers? To dine with Wong Dong? To discover cures for cancer, cruelty and loneliness? Is it too late? Maybe you should buy a watch.

BOSWELL. And yet I want to do all that. And much more. Everything, everything.

READER. Yet all this while, all this long while, you've never even looked at a pickle.

BOSWELL. A pickle? I've seen pickles.

READER. What kind?

BOSWELL. A — it was green.

READER. There're an awful lot of pickles. An awful lot of green ones. There are sweet pickles, garlic pickles, butter pickles, cucumber pickles, jalapeño pickles, midget pickles, gherkin pickles, kosher pickles, dot pickles, dill and baby dills. Whole shelves in stores hold nothing but pickles and we haven't even delved into your relish.

BOSWELL. Relish? Pickles? You've digressed. We were discussing something of import.

READER. I'm telling you, look to the pickle. Study its size, its shape, the colors, the smells, the ways it can be sliced. Take it into your heart. Sleep with it under your pillow. Walk with it in the dark.

BOSWELL. A pickle. Just one pickle.

READER. It's best not to spread yourself too thin. Write the word "pickle" ten thousand times in small, precise letters using green ink. That will be the start of everything.

BOSWELL. I — I can do that.

READER. I know you can.

BOSWELL. You — I — You ...

READER. What?

BOSWELL. You soothe me.

READER. Do I?

BOSWELL. Um. *(A beat.)* Tell me something about yourself. I want to know something personal.

READER. I have strange orbs.

BOSWELL. You do?

READER. Warm milk and blood and mud all flow from my orbs. Which do you want to suck?

BOSWELL. From your orbs? I — none. Thank you.

READER. It's a horrible situation for me. It makes me peculiar.

BOSWELL. I — yes. It's ...

READER. What?

BOSWELL. It's amazing to me how we all get by.

READER. I didn't know we all did.

BOSWELL. No, of course, *some* don't. *(He starts to leave, then turns to her.)* Pickle.

READER. Yes. And eat each pickle. Each pickle that you write. Taste it.

BOSWELL. Taste it.

READER. Yes. That's what I'd do.

BOSWELL. I'll do it then. I'll do it that way.

READER. Yes. Do. *(Boswell exits. Sound of a heartbeat. Reader twists like a viper as her breasts begin to ache. She clutches her right breast. It throbs with a painful longing, a longing for Boswell.)* Oh. God. Oh. God. Boswell. Boswell T-Thorp. Boswell. How long till you are mine? How long? *(As the lights fade, we hear L-Tip's desperate voice and the sound of a clock ticking.)*

L-TIP. *(Voice-over.)* God. Please. How long?

Scene 3

In front of the Pharmaceutical Distributors. Early morning. L-Tip is waiting for the store to open. She is distressed. She wears a black raincoat; no makeup; her hair is chaos.

L-TIP. Time. God. Time. *(Max enters. He is formally attired. It is the end of his evening. He wears a wilted laser flower in his lapel. As Max strides by, L-Tip reaches out to him.)* The time?

MAXWELL. Oh yes. Quarter till. *(Recognizing her.)* L-Tip.

38

L-TIP. *(Recognizing him.)* Max.

MAXWELL. How — why, how are you?

L-TIP. Oh, I'm standing outside the Pharmaceutical Distributors waiting for them to open so I can get my emotional equalizers, soul sedatives and pain executioners. That's how the fuck I am. How're you?

MAXWELL. Fine.

L-TIP. Just coming from the big bang-a-roo over at Cafe Who's Who?

MAXWELL. That's right.

L-TIP. Do tell.

MAXWELL. Umm. Look, I have a blue dot, if you ...

L-TIP. Thanks. I — good. Thanks. *(He gives her a blue dot.)* Max. I — those poems, I read. They were touching. You wrote some touching poems.

MAXWELL. I — was inspired. So.

L-TIP. Yeah. My marriage ended.

MAXWELL. I saw it on *Night Bites*.

L-TIP. Yeah? Well, it's a relief really. I mean, the only bad thing about the slice is now my career is, well, it's over. I'm through; I'm nicked; I'm glue rot. What time?

MAXWELL. Twelve till.

L-TIP. I don't know how this happened. I don't see how. I mean, I am a human being. I've tried my best. I study what to wear. I'm up on trends in music and restaurants; drugs and entertainment. I have all the up-to-date kitchen equipment. I thought if I got hold of all that, then other people wouldn't be mean to me. In fact, maybe I might even have this imperceivable right to be mean to them, just for not knowing or doing the things people who are worthwhile know and do. But, no. Uh-uh. Instead I'm the one who's being juiced out. It's me. Oh God, I'm so wretched and worthless; so swollen in salted, tormenting misery!

MAXWELL. There, there. Maybe you're just — you're probably having your — I mean ... Is this your ... ? Is it time for your ... ?

L-TIP. *(Cold and fierce.)* What?

MAXWELL. Nothing.

L-TIP. I know what you're suggesting, Max.

MAXWELL. No, no, I'm not.

L-TIP. Okay. Good. Don't. Even if — well, maybe I am. But that's not the point. There's some whole other point.

MAXWELL. I know. I know it's not the point. Hey. Listen. This'll be over. It'll pass. It's temporary.

L-TIP. Right. Like my whole life. It'll be over. It'll pass. While I just stand here, helplessly bleeding out one more egg, a child, a shell, an angel. Oh God. God. I'm having a weep-down. *(She starts to cry. Her tears are light blue in color.)*

MAXWELL. L-Tip, I didn't know you felt this way.

L-TIP. Oh, I don't. It's my hormones. They're the ones with feelings. As soon as they open up this spoon store, I'll fix it all out. *(She cries some more.)*

MAXWELL. I can't help it. I love to watch you cry. You're the only one I've ever known who cries blue tears.

L-TIP. Yeah. Well, too bad it doesn't earn me any K. What time?

MAXWELL. Six minutes. Look, I — *Celeb Bites* is doing a show on me. Maybe I could arrange for you to do the interview.

L-TIP. Me?

MAXWELL. Yeah.

L-TIP. A job?

MAXWELL. Yeah.

L-TIP. I'll take it. Time?

MAXWELL. *(Showing her his watch.)* Close.

L-TIP. *(Looking at his watch.)* Close. *(As the lights fade, we hear the sound of a clock ticking.)*

Scene 4

The boardwalk. The sound of a clock ticking continues. Reader is at her box. Her hair is neatly braided with a pink ribbon. She wears a sleeveless blouse. Incredible, long, black hair grows from her armpits. This hair is also neatly braided and tied with pink ribbon. She strokes her lips with the tip of this hair. She is waiting expectantly. The ocean roars. Sea birds squawk. Offshore machinery rumbles in the distance.

40

The sound of the clock ticking starts to fade as Boswell appears. He is walking with a cane. He is distracted yet ebullient. He carries a sheet of his handwriting. He spots Reader and waves the sheet at her.

BOSWELL. Ah ho! You were right. You knew. Pickles. Yes, pickles. It is coming to me for the first time in all this time. A torrential outpouring of creative bliss. I'm calling it, "Death and a Jar of Pickles." Compared to this, Boxdom is nothing more than puerile dribble. Why, if I can capture this poster, if it is fully grasped, it may be all we ever need to know. Finished! Done! Complete!

READER. You haven't said anything about my hair.

BOSWELL. Oh. No. Well, yes, I see. Now, about these universal pickles; these monolithic pickles — swimming and soaking in a sea of wretched, godless juices.

READER. Let me see the writing.

BOSWELL. *(Handing over the pages.)* Yes, of course. Pickle, pickle pickle.

READER. *(Looking over the pages of writing.)* Hmm. Very interesting.

BOSWELL. What?

READER. You're not whole. You're incomplete. Something is missing.

BOSWELL. What could be missing? I have my pickles. My poster. When it is complete, I'll have something to display. My masterpiece. I can hold it up to the whole world.

READER. And who will hold you back?

BOSWELL. Everyone. Everyone will be awed and amazed.

READER. Who will hold the real one? The one that feels and stinks and eats and can't sleep and gets so frightened by, by, by, by crashstorms and unpleasant faces and sores that don't heal in the cracks of his hands.

BOSWELL. What do you want from me? You know my condition. It's too late for all that. I have to be reasonable.

READER. Maybe it's time for you to blow your nose on the sleeve of reason.

BOSWELL. I don't know what you mean. Just tell me what to

41

write and it will be written.

READER. Feel my orbs. Both of them. Feel both of them. *(Boswell feels her breasts with his hands.)*

BOSWELL. *(With his hands on her breasts.)* Now please, you must tell me what to write.

READER. People come through the trees and look into your eyes. You stop them walking toward you. You stand still and shut your eyes.

BOSWELL. *(Averting his eyes and removing his hands from her breasts.)* I don't know that I do that.

READER. You do. *(Boswell looks at his hands. They are stained with blood and mud and milk.)* What's that on your hands?

BOSWELL. I — don't know.

READER. Look at it.

BOSWELL. It's nothing.

READER. Look.

BOSWELL. It's red and black ink stains.

READER. Where'd it come from?

BOSWELL. From a pen in my pocket. Tell me what to write.

READER. You tell me. Where did it come from? Who does it belong to? It doesn't smell like ink.

BOSWELL. Tell me what to write. Tell me. I'm telling you. If you can you should tell me now. *(He grabs her.)*

READER. Write the name of your beloved.

BOSWELL. I don't have a beloved.

READER. Write it one hundred times. *(He lets her go. She gasps for air.)* Where did it come from? Who does it belong to? It doesn't smell like ink.

BOSWELL. I don't have a beloved. *(Soul music comes up as the lights fade.)*

Scene 5

Boswell's apartment. Later that same day. C-Boy and William are dressed in costumes that are garish in a tawdry, makeshift sort of way. William wears a decorated orange splatter suit. They are rehearsing a lip-sync routine to a soulful love song filled with joyful longing and a hot beat; e.g., Jackie Wilson's "Lonely Teardrops."* William is struggling to keep up with C-Boy who, incredibly, is a dancing genius. He is capable of all sorts of fantastic feats. His emaciated body twists and turns like rubber. William attempts to spin into his arms and stumbles. C-Boy, the utter perfectionist, shakes his head dismally.

C-BOY. "No, no, no."

WILLIAM. I'll get it.

C-BOY. "Please observe." *(He demonstrates with a flourish.)*

WILLIAM. Okay. I see. More like this.*(She tries again. C-Boy nods his head in measured approval. He motions to her to try the step with him. They are in mid-spin when Boswell enters. They stop rehearsing immediately. William rushes to click off the music.)* Boswell, hello. I thought — I'm sorry.

BOSWELL. *(Distracted.)* Yes. Well, I have to — *(He wipes his soiled hands with a rag.)* These modern pens, they don't function. They malfunction. Inconvenient, all the mess.

WILLIAM. We thought you'd be working on your poster.

BOSWELL. What? No. I can't. It's been — you see there's no one to write down. I have no beloved.

WILLIAM. Well, I'm sorry. We'll get out of your way.

BOSWELL. What are you — your apparel is strange.

WILLIAM. These are our outfits. Tonight we perform in the Spectacular Splat Out Fund-Raiser. We're lip-syncing to an antique tune. C-Boy, he made up our whole dance. *(C-Boy beams*

* See Special Note on Songs and Recordings on copyright page.

in a strange, sheepish way.)
BOSWELL. Dance? You dance?
WILLIAM. He's very good. He taught me how.
BOSWELL. How what?
WILLIAM. To dance.
BOSWELL. Dance.
WILLIAM. Yes, if you wanted — I mean, we could show you.
BOSWELL. Show me? Why would I? You know I don't —
because I simply do not care for entertainment of any sort.
WILLIAM. Yes, well, we should go.
BOSWELL. All right. Do it. Go ahead. Let me see your dance. I
will watch it if I must.
WILLIAM. Okay. Yes. C-Boy, click it. *(C-boy clicks on the music,
and they do their dance. The gist of the dance is a crazed C-Boy beg-
ging, pleading, cajoling and romancing William to come back to him.
Boswell watches with gripped amazement. He finds himself totally
identifying with the demonic C-Boy, who is wholly possessed by
William and her relentless joy. The song ends. The dancers stop, then
slowly, almost sadly, they both look to Boswell for approval. Boswell sits
for a moment, stupefied.)*
BOSWELL. I — I — stunning. *(He rises to his feet and applauds.)*
Stunning. Hear, hear. Remarkable. I — hear, hear.
WILLIAM. *(Numb with shock.)* You liked it?
BOSWELL. Yes.
WILLIAM. Oh, C-Boy, he liked it. He liked it. *(William and
C-Boy hug each other joyfully. Boswell stands awkwardly alone.)*
Thank you, M. Boswell. Thank you. *(C-Boy salutes Boswell with
the Box Salute.)*
BOSWELL. I — you're welcome.
WILLIAM. Well, we should go on over. They want us there early.
They're gonna put us in rubber noses. *(C-Boy and William gather
their coats.)* Goodbye, Boswell, have a good night.
BOSWELL. I — when will you be back?
WILLIAM. Ten is the curfew.
BOSWELL. Ah, wait a minute.
WILLIAM. Yes?
BOSWELL. Good luck.
WILLIAM. *(Stunned and honored.)* Thanks. Thanks a lot, M.

Boswell. Thank you.

BOSWELL. Yes. Well. Bye.

WILLIAM. Bye. *(William and C-Boy start to leave.)*

BOSWELL. William?

WILLIAM. What?

BOSWELL. Could I come?

WILLIAM. Sure. Of course. Boswell's coming. You're coming.

BOSWELL. Yes, now let's go. Come on. We don't have all night. Put on your ears. You know how the temperature drops. *(They all three exit in a flurry. The lights start to fade as the* Celeb Bites' *theme music comes up.)*

Scene 6

Satellite station. The Celeb Bites' *theme music plays. L-Tip is interviewing Max on* Celeb Bites. *Max wears his charm suit and turban. He looks the perfect lost poet. L-Tip wears a dress made of different colored eyeglasses. She has green eyeglasses painted around her eyes. Her persona is that of the highly sexual intellectual. They both wear heavy makeup. A bright pink light burns down on them. The theme music dies down. L-Tip smiles into the camera.*

L-TIP. Welcome to *Celeb Bites.* I'm L-Tip the Hip Lip, your guest host. Tonight we are chewing it up with poet Maxwell T-Thorp, the man who is going to euth himself for love. Is he a romantic hero or a cowardly imbecile? Let's find out. Hello, Max.

MAXWELL. Hello, L-Tip.

L-TIP. So, tell us, Max, how long do you have?

MAXWELL. It's just a matter of completing the paperwork.

L-TIP. I hear the paperwork's appalling.

MAXWELL. Yes. Dreadful. It could take ... who knows?

L-TIP. Well, you fascinate me, M. T-Thorp. Tell us your story. How did you ever reach this point of desperation?

MAXWELL. I, well, I met her when we were very young. We went to school together. She'd sit at her terminal and make little cooing sounds. At recess one day she shared her soyball sandwich with me. Later we were married. I got a job at the Tank Bureau. I had half a cubicle, access to coffee dot, a key to the M. room, all your basic extra features. Then she divorced me. That's when I discovered, love can kill you.

L-TIP. And yet you sit here looking very zog. Your poems are today's craze. The laser show's in the works. I mean, aren't you being peculiarly short-eyed? Things change very rab in this world. Why, you could find a new love tomorrow. Or perhaps even tonight.

MAXWELL. I don't think so. You see, I'm not one of your twenty-first century use and cruisers who disposes of love like it was last meal's fuel frock.

L-TIP. Yet couldn't it be argued that you are wasting a life that should be cherished by committing this cowardly act of self-aggrandizement?

MAXWELL. I don't see that I'm wasting my life. In fact, just the opposite. Certainly to go on living would be the real coward's play. But I refuse to desecrate my profound love by adhering to the notion that it can be replaced, or forgotten, or lived without. I believe by dying I'm tipping my hat to life and the grand effect it can have on the living.

L-TIP. I'm sorry to say this but listening to you, I don't think you have any idea what real love is. Why, if you understood mature love, you would come to love and accept yourself and not degenerate into this destructive, distorted, masochistic indulgence.

MAXWELL. Yes, I'm afraid it's true. I don't know what real or mature love is. It's a mystery to me as I believe it is to most human beings. But the glorious thing is I dove instinctively into the splatter, having no idea how to swim, and now I'm going down for the third count and I have no regrets; the water is green and cool and I would rather be here than standing endlessly alone on the parched, dry shore.

L-TIP. I don't understand you. You never even treated her that well. This woman. I — I've done my research. And you pogoed around. You always pogoed around. You forgot her birthday eleven times. You ignored her at parties. You complained about the meals she clicked. You tore the arms off her Chee Chee Kitty.

MAXWELL. All the more reason. All the more reason to salvage the remnants of a love I shattered through reckless abuse.

L-TIP. But there you are again, only thinking of yourself. Why, she wouldn't want — any of this.

MAXWELL. How do you know?

L-TIP. I — she — we've talked.

MAXWELL. Yes. And what does she want?

L-TIP. She doesn't want you to euth yourself. She — she would take you back. If you did not do that.

MAXWELL. But does she...? Is she...? Could she love me still?

L-TIP. I — don't know. Things are so different. Everything.

MAXWELL. I can't go back without it. Always hoping for its return like sawed-off legs that will never grow back. Please. Tell me. What?

L-TIP. I — how can I? It's — you'll have to ask her.

MAXWELL. There's nothing to ask.

L-TIP. You're a charlatan. You're just doing this to sell your book. You'll call it off before it's over. *(To the camera.)* M.'s and M.'s that is my prediction.

MAXWELL. I understand your stupidity. You can't help it. You don't know her. The woman, I love. She's like no one else. She cries blue tears. *(They look at each other silently. We hear the sound of distant thunder as the lights fade.)*

Scene 7

Boswell's apartment. Night. Boswell walks with a cane. There is a nearly subliminal sound of distant thunder. C-Boy has been showing Boswell how to click a meal.

BOSWELL. So once more, I walk over there — *(He indicates the micromachine.)* I punch the top button, the red one, the one that

47

comes first. Then I remove my finger, and the meals will appear. *(C-Boy nods.)* I want to get this right. *(C-Boy starts to comb Boswell's hair.)* I hope she likes rainbow duck. It's a delicacy. Perhaps she doesn't like delicacies. I don't know. How should I know? *(C-Boy stops combing Boswell's hair. He removes a large hairball from the comb and tosses it into the receptacle. Boswell watches this with fine misery. He feels his thinning hair.)* Oh God. Hair is so much more attractive when it stays on the head. I'd better put on some more Hair Zap. How do my sores look? Are they very ugly? I — I shouldn't be doing this. This is all very silly. I'm going to change my mind in a minute. I'd better come to my senses. I'd better do it fast. *(Boswell exits into the lavatory. C-Boy goes to get his coat and ears. William enters. She wears her splatter suit and carries her helmet.)*

WILLIAM. C-Boy, hi. I — I'm so glad you're here. Where is he!? *(C-Boy motions to the lavatory.)* He's clicking dinner for me. Why do you think he's doing that? What do you think it means? *(C-Boy shrugs and heads for the door.)* Where are you going? *(C-Boy shows her a pass.)* Go. The recreation machine. Did he buy you that pass? *(C-Boy nods.)* Go. Go. What does this mean? He wants to see me alone. But why? What's going to happen? Oh, why is he clicking me dinner? *(C-Boy shrugs and exits. William takes off her orange parka. She is miserable with anticipation. Boswell comes out of the lavatory. He has sprayed black polish on his head. He walks with his cane.)*

BOSWELL. I don't know. I don't know. They should uninvent hair. It's nothing but a scourge. *(He realizes he is not talking to C-Boy.)* Oh. Ah … Has C-Boy … ? Gone?

WILLIAM. Um.

BOSWELL. Oh. Well. Are you ready for dinner?

WILLIAM. Uh-huh. *(Boswell walks with stiff self-consciousness over to the micromachine. He hesitates a moment, then punches a button. Gravel music plays loudly.)*

BOSWELL. I — I — that was the wrong button. A mistake has been made. Wait. Wait. *(Boswell punches several other buttons. The music stops, an alarm goes off. It rings frantically. He keeps pressing buttons. Finally, the alarm shuts off, the micromachine opens up, the dinners come out burnt and charred. Boswell looks at William with blank helplessness.)* I charred our dinners.

WILLIAM. Oh, well.

BOSWELL. Dinner is charred.

WILLIAM. I have a rancid carrot.

BOSWELL. A carrot. We can't be eating carrots. Not when I'm proposing marriage.

WILLIAM. You ... You're — marriage?

BOSWELL. Possibly.

WILLIAM. She's coming here?

BOSWELL. She's here. She's here. *(He points to her.)*

WILLIAM. Go.

BOSWELL. Don't answer. Please, don't answer. Not until — there are — I have some reasons. Number one: If my poster makes a big splash, you could be very rich. Number two: You know my condition; I won't last long; so even if it is a bad marriage, at least it will be short. Number three: You're already living here anyway. Number four: They have those super safe sex kits now. Everyone is using them, even healthy people. They say the results make nature a thing of the past. This would be so much better if I hadn't charred the meals. If the meals were sitting here like I had planned. *(There is the sound of thunder approaching.)* Oh, my God. A crashstorm. Thunder. I hate those things.

WILLIAM. Boswell —

BOSWELL. Please. You don't have to answer now. Just take your time. Think it over.

WILLIAM. There are things — I could never — Boswell —

BOSWELL. *(Overlapping from "I could ... ")* Please, I cannot hear an answer now. Not with the storm. Not tonight. *(The sound of thunder grows louder.)* Oh God, there's thunder. I hate it so much.

WILLIAM. *(Overlapping from "thunder")* You must listen — I have to — it's wrong — I'm wrong —

BOSWELL. *(Overlapping from "have")* Please — don't. The rain. Don't.

WILLIAM. You think I'm nice, but I'm not. I used to kill animals, little animals. I liked to kill them. It made me feel in charge, like I was the boss or a Being, a real high Being. That was a long time ago, but it's still inside me. And I don't know what to do. It will always have been done. *(She stands before him, stricken. He longs to comfort her but is afraid he doesn't know how.)*

BOSWELL. Please. It's ... Don't. You were young. It's forgotten.

Believe me. I swear to you. None of that matters. I want you with me. You are my beloved. Just please now. Please. *(He finally puts his arm around her. The thunder rages. Rain pours down. He holds her tightly. She holds him back.)* Oh God, the thunder. Are you scared of thunder?

WILLIAM.   No. Nothing. Now. I'm not scared of nothing. *(They hold each other as the rain pours down in torrents and the thunder clashes. As the lights fade, beautiful green rain appears on the TVP screen.)*

Scene 8

The boardwalk. It is sunset. The sky is orange and green. Waves are crashing. Thunder rumbles. Lightning flashes. The Reader is tearing apart her box. Her shirt is torn, exposing her breasts. Her left breast is caked with mud, her right with blood. Her hair and beard are tangled and bedraggled. Boswell appears. He clings to a sheet of paper.

BOSWELL.   Reader! Reader! Where are you? Her name. I have her name. My beloved. Reader! Reader. I — what's happened to you?

READER.   I can no longer bear the overwhelming stench of other people's lives. I'm closing up shop.

BOSWELL.   You've helped me so much. You see, I never thought — but sometimes when I'm with her, I forget, I don't remember. There's only us. Would you like to see her name? *(He offers the paper to her.)*

READER.   I don't have to. I can smell it. Please. *(She waves the paper away.)* A splatterer from the CTZ. The rancid smell of her stubby hands.

BOSWELL.   She works very hard.

READER.   Of course. Don't despair. You've done what you have done.

BOSWELL.   I — I've never been so happy. We'll start the defrost

on her kids, then plan the wedding. She wants an orange dress. If the kids thaw in time, they can be there. I'll buy them orange suits. Later I'll have to teach them all to read and write and clap to music. The alphabet is important. I'll make certain they learn how to cross their T's with vigor and hope. I'm sure it can all be done.
READER. No, I wouldn't worry about the poster.
BOSWELL. The poster. No. I can always mark out some time.
READER. Your sores are red now. Time is ticking.
BOSWELL. *(He looks at his sores; they have turned blood-red.)* Well, it was really just some pickles.
READER. Exactly.
BOSWELL. I thought perhaps it could have been good.
READER. Your best. Your signature.
BOSWELL. My signature. But still it's not that important. I mean, after all, she, William, she is the one.
READER. And it would have been such pressure for her being a great man's wife. People might question her. They might not understand your reasons for choosing an unattractive, uneducated, dim-witted splatterer from the CTZ with frozen children that are not even your own. You know; people talk.
BOSWELL. Still, I'm thinking even so, she is the one. Look at the writing. I'm sure it's all there. *(He hands the sheet of paper out to her.)*
READER. You're sure?
BOSWELL. Yes.
READER. You're very sure.
BOSWELL. I — yes.
READER. Then why are you asking me?
BOSWELL. To be … to be certain … I have to be certain. *(The Reader takes the paper from him and looks at it for a long moment.)*
READER. M. William Smit. No, she's not the one. You've made a mistake. A mistake has been made. *(She hands the sheet of paper back to Boswell. He takes it in his hand and hobbles on his cane in a ghostlike trance. The sunset fades. The sky turns dark.)*

51

Scene 9

Boswell's apartment. William is wearing a frilly orange dress and has orange dandies in her hair. Boswell enters. His face is white. He looks at the red sores that have appeared on his skin.

WILLIAM. Hello.

BOSWELL. Hello.

WILLIAM. My dress arrived.

BOSWELL. Yes, it's very nice.

WILLIAM. Thank you for giving it to me. It makes me — it's beautiful. *(The TVP begins to bleep. Boswell clicks it up. An official appears on the screen. C-Boy is with him.)*

BOSWELL. *(To the official on the screen.)* Yes? Hello.

OFFICIAL. *(On the screen.)* I wanted to inform you that we have retrieved your x-ward, M. C-Boy K-Trill, on his food box pickup. He is officially reinstated as a full-time Gov. ward. You have no further obligations concerning this case.

BOSWELL. Yes. Fine.

OFFICIAL. H.A.N.D. *(Boswell clicks off the TVP screen.)*

WILLIAM. They've got C-Boy.

BOSWELL. Yes. I've returned him. *(He goes back to his writing.)*

WILLIAM. But why?

BOSWELL. I can't do everything.

WILLIAM. They're gonna — they'll put him back on the streets.

BOSWELL. He'll have his food box. He'll be no worse off than he was before.

WILLIAM. Please, you can't — we have to think about this.

BOSWELL. When did we start thinking together?

WILLIAM. We don't — I didn't mean —

BOSWELL. You didn't mean what?

WILLIAM. I don't know.

BOSWELL. You don't know what?

WILLIAM. Nothing.

BOSWELL. Yes, well, there it is. Don't you see how impossible this is. You don't know anything. You have no idea how to think. It simply is not something you do on a regular basis. I mean, can you tell me — have you ever wondered — what is your purpose?
WILLIAM. Uh-uh.
BOSWELL. That doesn't surprise me. And yet it seems apparent that, if you are going to be alive, you should know your purpose. But you don't know. You don't even think. See how we are incapable of having any sort of intelligent, meaningful exchange!
WILLIAM. I thought — it seemed — you do love me.
BOSWELL. Did I ever say that? When did I say that? I do not recall saying that.
WILLIAM. You don't have to say.
BOSWELL. Well, if I don't say, if I didn't say, what made you think — excuse me, I forgot, you don't think. So I suppose I have to stand here and explain everything to you. Well, get this flat. Love is a mendacious myth. Everyone is just an egg. A slimy yolk in their own shell. Smash two eggs together, what happens? They break. The result is two chickens are killed, a runny omelette is served, "Good morning, everyone." H.A.N. fucking D.
WILLIAM. You want to call off the marriage?
BOSWELL. I think, perhaps.
WILLIAM. All right.
BOSWELL. I'm going to devote myself entirely to the pickle.
WILLIAM. I — I.
BOSWELL. What?
WILLIAM. I'll fix you a medical concoction.
BOSWELL. It's not time.
WILLIAM. But, I see — your sores, they're —
BOSWELL. What?
WILLIAM. Red.
BOSWELL. I think you should leave.
WILLIAM. Leave?
BOSWELL. Yes. I don't want you around me while I'm dying. I know how you like to kill and torture dying prey. It's part of your makeup. It's who you are. It makes you feel good. Like you're a Being, a real high Being.
WILLIAM. Oh no, no. Don't. I can't. I'll go. I'll pack. *(She starts*

to pack.) I'll go. I — where? If only — I just — I — I wanna go home. I do. But it's — all gone. My home. My family, the silk elm, the red saucer I ate from. And my brother, Andy. How fast he could run across the dirt. How he recited to me such things he would write if ever he could learn to read. I want so much to go see my home. I do. I do. I wish I could dream it all back.

BOSWELL. Yes, yes, you can't go home again. You'd know that if you had an education. But you don't, so you have to learn everything through personal experience. It must be so exhausting. Do you have all of your things?

WILLIAM. Yes.

BOSWELL. Then you should go. *(William picks up all of her belongings and exits.)* Good then. She's gone. Now I can work. Back to the pickle. My signature. *(Boswell goes back to his writing. William walks in the road alone. She is full of passion and rage.)*

WILLIAM. You will not have my heart. You cannot keep it. I need it inside me.

Scene 10

Celeb Bites *theme music comes up. A huge poster shaped like a pickle comes up on the TVP screen. The poster is covered with a tarp. Various highbrows are eyeing it with anticipation. Lights come up on a grassy knoll. Day. L-Tip is interviewing Boswell. A harsh, pink light encircles them. L-Tip wears a skin-tight dress and a peculiar headdress that bobbles. Boswell has lost most of his hair. He stands with two canes. His sores are black now, but his eyes are still burning. The* Celeb Bites' *music starts to fade.*

L-TIP. Hello, this is L-Tip the Hip Lip and I'm standing here with art philosopher, M. Boswell T-Thorp. Any moment now the A.P. Bureau Chiefs will be unveiling M. T-Thorp's new poster, "Death and a Jar of Pickles." Are you nervous, M. T-Thorp?

BOSWELL. Not in the least. In fact, I've never been so relaxed in my entire life.

L-TIP. May I ask, why you have chosen to retreat to this grassy knoll rather than to be present at the Show All Pavilion to see how your poster is publicly received?

BOSWELL. Well, L-Tip, I'll tell you, I love the public. They're all wonderful folks, I'm sure. But I really have no interest in their opinions. I'm secure and fulfilled in who I am. My poster stands on its own.

L-TIP. Well, M. T-Thorp, you certainly are a man of Himalayan values.

BOSWELL. Yes, well, if you like.

L-TIP. Thank you for talking to us. It's been a true bang-a-roo. And please, H.A.N.D.

BOSWELL. H.A.N.D.? *(The pink circle of light abruptly disappears.)*

L-TIP. *(Talking to the crew.)* Okay, fine. Click. Were you able to get in all of my headgear? Sin. Now let's pack up and dust to the Show All.

BOSWELL. *(Coming up to her.)* I thought you were going to ask me for my interpretation of the poster. Why, that interview was vulgarly anorexic and evisceratingly inane!

L-TIP. Please, Boswell, don't start giving me shit. I've just spent the entire morning trying to suck in my stomach.

BOSWELL. You think just because you have your own satellite show — why, I'm getting ready to take this world by storm. When people see these pickles, nothing will ever be the same. There may well be a referendum to reinstate the office of king. *(Max enters; he is horribly distressed.)*

MAXWELL. There you are — I — have you heard?

BOSWELL. What?

MAXWELL. Your poster? The unveiling?

BOSWELL. No.

MAXWELL. Don't go down there. It's — they didn't —

BOSWELL. What? It's not good. I can see this isn't good. *(L-Tip clicks in her portable TVP.)*

L-TIP. *(Into the TVP remote.)* Stringer-K, are you down there? What's going on? Pan over. *(She watches the action on the tiny TVP screen.)* Oh my God. They're throwing things at your pickle.

BOSWELL. Things? What things?

L-TIP. Fruit cores, chairs, mud balls. Look at this, an evil pork is setting it on fire.

BOSWELL. Oh, my God. My poor pickles. Stop them. Won't somebody stop them? Won't the Stick Guards — won't they stop them?

L-TIP. Looks like the Stick Guards are in on it, too. Why, they're beating on it with spiked mallets.

BOSWELL. My precious poster. My dearest pickles. Why? Oh, why?

MAXWELL. I don't know, I heard they thought it was making fun of our Food Suppliers.

BOSWELL. Our Food Suppliers??!! But I wasn't — I didn't — this was not a joke. This was not in fun. I wanted the people, I wanted them to understand my pickles. Their thoughts, their feelings, their predicament. What it was like for them inside that jar!!

L-TIP. Stabilize. Stabilize. Remember what you said about your work standing on its own? How you are secure and fulfilled in who you are?

BOSWELL. Lies. All lies. Nothing but lies.

L-TIP. Try to equalize. I've got to go down there.

MAXWELL. *(To L-Tip.)* Nice suit.

L-TIP. Drop dead. *(L-Tip hurries off.)*

MAXWELL. Hey, look. I'm sorry, Boz. I'm really sorry. But I suppose if you were, well, grasping at straws, you might see it as something of a compliment that the people would take the time to so brutally and viciously destroy your work.

BOSWELL. Yes, well, why don't we just leave that chaff in the crib.

MAXWELL. Sure, of course. *(A beat.)* Well … isn't it strange.

BOSWELL. What?

MAXWELL. We're both … standing here. *(Boswell looks at Max standing on the grassy knoll. He then becomes horribly aware of his own body standing on the surface of the world. Slowly, Boswell starts to breathe very heavily. Max tries to grin, but he seems to lack sincerity. As the lights fade, cheerful piped-in euth music comes up.)*

Scene 11

Euthanasia Gardens. Flowery euth music plays. L-Tip enters. She wears a red coat decorated with hearts and a red hat with a veil. She carries a TVP remote. William enters dressed in her orange dress, which has been dyed red. She wears her W.Y. badge. She also wears a TVP remote.

WILLIAM. Hi.

L-TIP. William.

WILLIAM. Hi.

L-TIP. It's been ...

WILLIAM. Yes. Long.

L-TIP. Where's C-Boy? I heard he's become your ward.

WILLIAM. Yes, he has. He'll be here today. After I come, he's coming. We're trading off staying with my kids. They're in final thaw.

L-TIP. Oh, brill. That's just brill.

WILLIAM. Yes. It's been a very fortunate time for me. I got elected Worker of the Year. Plus we won a bonus vacation to anyplace in the zone that hasn't been splattered.

L-TIP. Oh. Where will you go?

WILLIAM. Anaheim. We've already made reservations to see that famous ceiling they brought over.

L-TIP. What ceiling?

WILLIAM. The one with all sorts of old-fashioned, heavyset people painted on it. I think it's got God in it somewhere and he's going like this — *(William reaches her arm out and extends her index finger.)*

L-TIP. Oh, yes. That's very popular.

WILLIAM. Uh-huh. *(A beat.)* Is he — I mean — have you seen Boswell?

L-TIP. No. He's not here yet.

WILLIAM. Do you know how he is?

L-TIP. Not good. His sores are black now.

WILLIAM. Oh. I just — I hope I can leave before he comes. I don't ever wanna see him again. Why are we waiting?

L-TIP. The body's being capsulized. It shouldn't be much longer.

WILLIAM. Umm. Would you like to see my kids?

L-TIP. Oh yes.

WILLIAM. I'll click them up. *(William takes her remote TVP and clicks through her number.)*

WILLIAM. *(Into the TVP.)* C-Boy, it's me. Look who's here. *(L-Tip waves into William's TVP screen.)*

L-TIP. Hi, C-Boy. Jacka, jacka.

WILLIAM. *(Into the TVP.)* C-Boy, show her the kids. Look, there they are.

L-TIP. Oh. Oh. Aren't they shug.

WILLIAM. *(Pointing at the screen.)* That one's Bonnie. And that's Tabell. Look how they can move their hands and toes. In just about a week their lids will start to open.

L-TIP. Sin. Simply, sin.

WILLIAM. *(Into the TVP.)* Thanks, C-Boy. I'll be back as soon as I can. H.A.N.D. *(She clicks off.)*

L-TIP. I — did you know I have a child now?

WILLIAM. No.

L-TIP. Yes, I've been desperate for one for a long time. Here, I'll click her up. *(She clicks through her number.)* Her name's Grace. *(Into her TVP.)* Yes, H.K., please put Grace on the TVP.

WILLIAM. *(Looking at L-Tip's TVP screen.)* Oh, she's very pretty.

L-TIP. Isn't she the cutest and most cuddly. She's the newest thing. They call them Toss 'Em Toddlers. Her natural life span is only three years. Isn't it wonderful. She'll be adorable her whole life. And I won't ever have to worry about those awkward years. Not to mention the high cost of education. *(L-Tip waves goodbye to Grace and clicks her off.)*

WILLIAM. Won't it be sad though?

L-TIP. Oh no. It's all completely natural. See, I don't have time for a full-term child. I mean, I'm competing in a world where fantasy puppets set the step. They never take time out for children or family, ultra surgery or even rehab. They're completely consumed with constructing careers. The pressure gets to be devastating. Of course, I'm terrifically unhappy. Before I started going to my therochief I never even suspected how unhappy I was. Now I'm totally aware of my misery. It's a big improvement. *(Reader appears in a white dress decorated with pink carnations. She has shaved her beard and her hair is neatly bubbled and coiffed. Her demeanor has completely changed. She is vapid, calm and glazed.)*

READER. Good morning M.'s. The capsulation of Maxwell T-Thorp has been completed. His inscription, "Love and death; no regrets." Please come view.

L-TIP. Thanks. *(L-Tip and William head towards the entrance.)* God, don't we look silly. I hate these theme funerals. *(They all three exit. Boswell enters. He walks with two canes. His black sores have spread. He slowly hobbles to the bench and sits down. William reenters. She is wiping away tears. Boswell sees her.)*

BOSWELL. Hello.

WILLIAM. Hi.

BOSWELL. Did you go in?

WILLIAM. Yes. Yes. Max. Poor Max. He's so small. They've made him so small.

BOSWELL. They've capsulized him?

WILLIAM. Yes, but he's, well, they've got him smiling. It's this small, little, tiny, little smile.

BOSWELL. Well, they do that, I suppose.

WILLIAM. Uh-huh.

BOSWELL. William.

WILLIAM. What?

BOSWELL. I thought I might never see you again.

WILLIAM. Yes, I thought so, too.

BOSWELL. Would you shake my hand?

WILLIAM. Why?

BOSWELL. I don't know. No rock feelings?

WILLIAM. But I do; I have them. I have rock feelings.

BOSWELL. Well, then, I don't know. What is there to do? It's all too late. What is there to do?

WILLIAM. I have to go.

BOSWELL. Yes, well, H.A.N.D. *(William exits. Reader enters. She approaches Boswell.)*

READER. Hello. Would you like me to show you to the viewing room? The capsule is on display.

BOSWELL. No. Not just yet.

READER. Take your time. *(Reader strolls around the garden. He watches her.)*

BOSWELL. Excuse me. But do I know you?

READER. Me? I don't think so.

BOSWELL. There's something about you. You remind me ... Did you ever have a beard?

READER. Yes, I think, perhaps. You see, I was very ill at one point. I've had brain fiber treatments. I'm much better now.

BOSWELL. What was — the problem?

READER. I was malignantly insane. I thought I could read people's lives through their handwriting. I'd take people's "K" and spin deluded tales. I made one pathetic man write the word "pickle" ten thousand times. But I'm much better now.

BOSWELL. Then you — it was all — you never knew ... anything?

READER. What could I know? I was crippled with a fevered cranium.

BOSWELL. Oh my God. Oh my God. A mistake has been made. *(L-Tip enters. She is crying blue tears.)*

L-TIP. Max. Dear Max. God. How can I live without him? How can I ever live without him? Boswell —

BOSWELL. It's too late! *(Boswell rises to his feet and hobbles in the same direction William departed.)*

L-TIP. Yes. But I did ... I realize now, I did love him. I loved him all along. *(Boswell stops. He is gasping for air. He points one of his canes in William's direction, trembling with determination.)*

BOSWELL. It's too late though!

L-TIP. Yes, all along. I loved him all along. *(Boswell lowers his cane.)*

READER. I have to believe. I am; I'm much better now.

BOSWELL. William! My beloved! William! *(Boswell moves forward and goes to find William. The lights fade to blackout.)*

End of Play

PROPERTY LIST

Television phone and remote
Portable television phone
Square shirt (BOSWELL)
Square tie (BOSWELL)
Square shoes (BOSWELL)
Square wig (BOSWELL)
Square belt (BOSWELL)
Ear fuel (MAX, L-TIP)
Day-Glo tickets (L-TIP)
Two vials of red liquid (L-TIP)
Shoes (WILLIAM)
Blue dot (L-TIP, MAX)
List (L-TIP, BOSWELL)
Galaxy satellite (L-TIP)
Medical concoction (WILLIAM)
Glass (WILLIAM)
Blood (MAX)
White bow tie (WILLIAM)
White gloves (WILLIAM)
White visor (WILLIAM)
White shoes (WILLIAM)
Box (WILLIAM)
Laser remote (WILLIAM, L-TIP)
Two micro meals (WILLIAM)
Tomato (BOSWELL)
Food box (C-BOY)
Pieces of paper (MAY)
Air contraption (L-TIP)
Box of memorabilia (BOSWELL)
Strange creature (WILLIAM)
Wire brush (WILLIAM)
Letter chip (BOSWELL)
Blue Dot cactus (JENNIFER)
Square button with Boswell's face on it (BOSWELL)
Laser tray (BOSWELL)
Receptacle (BOSWELL)

Food (L-TIP)
Drug vials (L-TIP)
Grapes (L-TIP)
Red Dogs (L-TIP)
Laser ring (L-TIP)
Stool (READER)
Laser pen (READER, BOSWELL)
Quarter (BOSWELL)
Book galleys (MAX)
Laser stick (C-BOY)
Backpack (WILLIAM)
Boots (WILLIAM)
Pages of paper (READER, MAX)
Watch (MAX)
Canes (BOSWELL)
Blood (READER)
Mud (READER)
Milk (READER)
Rag (BOSWELL)
Comb (C-BOY)
Hairball (C-BOY)
Coat (C-BOY)
Ears (C-BOY)
Helmet (WILLIAM)
Pass (C-BOY)
Parka (WILLIAM)
Two dinners (BOSWELL)
Miscellaneous belongings (WILLIAM)

SOUND EFFECTS

Bleeping
Sounds of a cocktail party
Street noise
Wind
Trash being blown down alleyways
Animals howling
Rushing water
Shower
Doorbell
Ocean
Loud buzz
Banging on door
Carnival noises
Clean-up crews' machinery
Buzz noise
Heartbeat
Clock ticking
Seabirds
Offshore machinery
Soul music
TV show theme music
Thunder
Gravel music
Alarm
Rain
Euth music

NEW PLAYS

★ **THE CIDER HOUSE RULES, PARTS 1 & 2 by Peter Parnell, adapted from the novel by John Irving.** Spanning eight decades of American life, this adaptation from the Irving novel tells the story of Dr. Wilbur Larch, founder of the St. Cloud's, Maine orphanage and hospital, and of the complex father-son relationship he develops with the young orphan Homer Wells. "...luxurious digressions, confident pacing...an enterprise of scope and vigor..." –*NY Times.* "...The fact that I can't wait to see Part 2 only begins to suggest just how good it is..." –*NY Daily News.* "...engrossing...an odyssey that has only one major shortcoming: It comes to an end." –*Seattle Times.* "...outstanding...captures the humor, the humility...of Irving's 588-page novel..." –*Seattle Post-Intelligencer.* [9M, 10W, doubling, flexible casting] PART 1 ISBN: 0-8222-1725-2 PART 2 ISBN: 0-8222-1726-0

★ **TEN UNKNOWNS by Jon Robin Baitz.** An iconoclastic American painter in his seventies has his life turned upside down by an art dealer and his ex-boyfriend. "...breadth and complexity...a sweet and delicate harmony rises from the four cast members...Mr. Baitz is without peer among his contemporaries in creating dialogue that spontaneously conveys a character's social context and moral limitations..." –*NY Times.* "...darkly funny, brilliantly desperate comedy...TEN UNKNOWNS vibrates with vital voices." –*NY Post.* [3M, 1W] ISBN: 0-8222-1826-7

★ **BOOK OF DAYS by Lanford Wilson.** A small-town actress playing St. Joan struggles to expose a murder. "...[Wilson's] best work since *Fifth of July*...An intriguing, prismatic and thoroughly engrossing depiction of contemporary small-town life with a murder mystery at its core...a splendid evening of theater..." –*Variety.* "...fascinating...a densely populated, unpredictable little world." –*St. Louis Post-Dispatch.* [6M, 5W] ISBN: 0-8222-1767-8

★ **THE SYRINGA TREE by Pamela Gien.** Winner of the 2001 Obie Award. A breathtakingly beautiful tale of growing up white in apartheid South Africa. "Instantly engaging, exotic, complex, deeply shocking...a thoroughly persuasive transport to a time and a place...stun[s] with the power of a gut punch..." –*NY Times.* "Astonishing...affecting ...[with] a dramatic and heartbreaking conclusion...A deceptive sweet simplicity haunts THE SYRINGA TREE..." –*A.P.* [1W (or flexible cast)] ISBN: 0-8222-1792-9

★ **COYOTE ON A FENCE by Bruce Graham.** An emotionally riveting look at capital punishment. "The language is as precise as it is profane, provoking both troubling thought and the occasional cheerful laugh...will change you a little before it lets go of you." –*Cincinnati CityBeat.* "...excellent theater in every way..." –*Philadelphia City Paper.* [3M, 1W] ISBN: 0-8222-1738-4

★ **THE PLAY ABOUT THE BABY by Edward Albee.** Concerns a young couple who have just had a baby and the strange turn of events that transpire when they are visited by an older man and woman. "An invaluable self-portrait of sorts from one of the few genuinely great living American dramatists...rockets into that special corner of theater heaven where words shoot off like fireworks into dazzling patterns and hues." –*NY Times.* "An exhilarating, wicked...emotional terrorism." –*NY Newsday.* [2M, 2W] ISBN: 0-8222-1814-3

★ **FORCE CONTINUUM by Kia Corthron.** Tensions among black and white police officers and the neighborhoods they serve form the backdrop of this discomfiting look at life in the inner city. "The creator of this intense...new play is a singular voice among American playwrights...exceptionally eloquent..." –*NY Times.* "...a rich subject and a wise attitude." –*NY Post.* [6M, 2W, 1 boy] ISBN: 0-8222-1817-8

DRAMATISTS PLAY SERVICE, INC.
440 Park Avenue South, New York, NY 10016 212-683-8960 Fax 212-213-1539
postmaster@dramatists.com   www.dramatists.com